KITTEN TRAINING

AND CRITTERS, TOO!

KITTEN TRAINING
AND CRITTERS, TOO!

JUDY PETERSON-FLEMING
AND BILL FLEMING

PHOTOGRAPHS BY DARRYL BUSH

TAMBOURINE BOOKS, NEW YORK

FOR OUR RAY OF SUNSHINE, CIERA

acknowledgments

The authors would like to thank the animals and trainers of Marine World Africa USA, a unique wildlife park and oceanarium in Vallejo, California, for their help.

Since 1968, Marine World has introduced the wonders of the animal world to over 28 million visitors, including 12 million children spanning two generations. The park features animals of land, sea, and air in show performances, innovative exhibits, participatory attractions, and remarkable one-on-one encounters between animals, trainers, and guests.

Marine World Africa USA serves as a showcase for the many wonderful relationships that can exist between humans and animals. The park is owned by the Marine World Foundation, a nonprofit organization devoted to furthering people's understanding and appreciation of our world's wildlife.

We would also like to thank all of the children photographed in this book. Their patience and closeness to their pets made this book possible.

Finally, thanks to Brian and Cameron Reingold-Reiss, for letting Deb use her creativity!

note to parents

Training a kitten is an experience that can bring the whole family closer together. Just as the trainers in this book work as a team while training

exotic animals, your family will need to work together to train your new pet. Everyone in the family can become involved. Even the youngest children can participate by repeating the commands, such as saying "No" when the cat jumps up on the counter.

Your children will learn many interesting facts about wild animals while learning how to train their kitten. It will be exciting to them to use the same methods that trainers use with exotic animals.

It is important to remember that a trained pet is well behaved and can participate in family fun. Training your kitten is a great family activity that will give you greater enjoyment of your pet.

NOW THAT YOU KNOW HOW TO CARE FOR YOUR KITTEN, IT'S TIME TO LEARN HOW TO TRAIN YOUR PET. SEEING HOW TRAINERS WORK WITH WILD ANIMALS WILL HELP. ONCE YOU HAVE TRAINED YOUR KITTEN, YOU WILL ENJOY BEING TOGETHER EVEN MORE.

CATS CAN SEE SIX TIMES BETTER IN DIM LIGHT THAN PEOPLE CAN.

A kitten should be trained to listen to you, so you can enjoy each other's company in many situations. If you follow the simple instructions in this book, you can learn how to train your kitten. Before starting, your kitten needs to become familiar with you. A good way is to let her sniff your hand and get to know your scent. During training, you and your kitten will become best friends and will be able to do many other things together.

critters, too!

This trainer has been training Pancho, a young llama, for several years. Llamas in the wild would be afraid to come close to a person, but Pancho now completely trusts his trainer. Because he is trained, they can go all around the park and run and play in many areas together. This trainer uses many of the same methods to train Pancho that you will use to train your kitten.

LLAMAS COME FROM THE HIGH MOUNTAINS OF SOUTH AMERICA. THEIR LONG SHAGGY COATS KEEP THEM WARM IN COLD WEATHER.

WHEN KITTENS' BACK LEGS ARE STRONG ENOUGH, THEY WILL STAND AND "HOP" TOWARD THEIR MOTHER TO GREET HER.

Go very *s-l-o-w-l-y* while training your kitten. Kittens can be very nervous, especially when you first start to work together. If you try to rush your kitten, she will only get confused, and it will take longer for her to learn new tasks.

When this trainer works with Mara, she takes each step very slowly. The cheetah will have to try new behaviors several times before she understands what the trainer really wants her to do. Because the trainer never hurries Mara, learning new things is fun for all, and Mara actually learns much faster.

UNLIKE LIONS AND TIGERS, CHEETAHS PURR JUST THE WAY YOUR KITTEN DOES— ONLY MUCH LOUDER!

CATS WALK ON THEIR TOES, WHICH ALLOWS THEM TO MOVE FASTER THAN IF THEY WALKED FLAT ON THEIR PAWS.

Animals learn best by doing the same things over and over. When training your kitten, you will need to repeat an exercise many times. Pick *one* word as the command for each behavior that you teach your kitten. That word will be *repeated* many times during the training. For instance, this boy kneels several feet away from his kitten with treats in his hand. He says "Come" several times to the kitten while teaching her how to come to him. He *never* changes the word to "Here" or to the kitten's name, but always uses the same command. This way the kitten quickly learns what the command means. The average cat can understand twenty-five to fifty words.

Stormy has learned many different behaviors from her trainers, and knows exactly what they want her to do. When this dolphin was learning a behavior, her trainers would have her do it over and over, many times. They always used the same commands.

A DOLPHIN'S SKIN IS VERY SMOOTH AND FEELS JUST LIKE A WET INNER TUBE.

A CAT USES ITS WHISKERS AS FEELERS TO TELL WHETHER A GAP IS WIDE ENOUGH TO SQUEEZE THROUGH.

Always use a gentle but *firm* voice when giving your kitten a command. You should *never* yell commands at your kitten, as this will only scare him and make it very difficult for him to learn. The voice you use when giving your kitten commands should be very different from the voice you use when playing with or praising your kitten.

Grendel's trainer always uses a gentle but firm voice, so that the young alligator knows that the trainer is serious, but does not become afraid. Grendel has learned to listen to the trainer because his voice is always gentle and never harsh.

AN ALLIGATOR GROWS TEETH CONTINUALLY THROUGHOUT ITS LIFE.

WHEN YOUR KITTEN IS HAPPY AND RELAXED, ITS EARS POINT FORWARD AND SLIGHTLY OUTWARD.

Always reward your kitten after she has done what you've asked her to do, so that she knows she's done it right. Tell her how well she has done by giving her one of her favorite treats, along with several loving hugs and pats. Rewarding your kitten will make training enjoyable for her, so she will always want to do more.

and critters, too!

Vigga, a killer whale, is being given mackerel, her favorite fish treat. Vigga loves learning new behaviors from her trainer because she always gets a toy or treat or her favorite reward—a rubdown!

KILLER WHALES CAN EAT OVER 150 POUNDS OF FISH A DAY!

CATS WILL TWITCH THEIR TAILS WHEN THEY ARE IN A STATE OF CONFUSION OVER A DECISION THEY NEED TO MAKE. ONCE THE DECISION IS MADE, THE TAIL WILL STOP TWITCHING.

Training should be enjoyable for you and your kitten, so keep the training time short. Watch your kitten for signs that he is losing interest, such as looking away or acting restless. Stop the training session as soon as you see these signs of boredom. If your kitten loses interest in the lesson, he will not enjoy the training as much and will not be as excited to start again next time.

critters, too!

A HARBOR SEAL'S FRONT FLIPPERS HAVE VERY SHARP CLAWS.

This trainer watches Wilbur, a harbor seal, closely while they work together. If Wilbur is enjoying himself and showing a lot of interest, the trainer keeps going. As soon as Wilbur shows signs of getting bored, the trainer will end that session, just as you should do with your kitten.

FALLING CATS ALWAYS
LAND ON THEIR FEET. THAT'S
BECAUSE THEY HAVE A
TWISTING INSTINCT THAT
TURNS THEM TO THEIR FEET
BEFORE THEY EVER HIT
THE GROUND.

Teaching your kitten "No" is very important. Whenever your kitten is doing something you don't want her to, say "No" in a firm, gentle voice. Always use the same word and the same tone of voice. It will confuse your kitten if you say other words, like "Stop" or "Don't."

Jake knows he has done something wrong when the trainer tells him "No," because he was taught this word when he was very young. Jake does not get confused, because his trainer always uses the same word and repeats it many times whenever he does something wrong.

CAMELS CAN GO FOR LONG PERIODS OF TIME WITHOUT WATER—UP TO TEN MONTHS IF THEY AREN'T WORKING!

A CAT MAY "HISS" WHEN IT FEELS THREATENED OR ANGRY, BY OPENING ITS MOUTH WIDE. THE SOUND MAY BE TO IMITATE A SNAKE, AS A SIGNAL THAT THE CAT TOO CAN BE DANGEROUS.

You can teach your kitten *never* to have his claws out around you, so you won't get scratched. Do this by gently tapping your kitten's paws and saying a stern "No" every time your kitten's claws come out. If you do this *every* time your kitten's claws come out, he will soon learn to keep them in when you're around. This becomes more important as he gets older, and his claws get bigger and sharper.

This trainer is gently tapping Nikka's large paw while telling her "No" for having her claws out. Although Nikka learned this when she was a few months old, she needs to be reminded now and then. Because of the training Nikka has received, the trainer never gets scratched. This makes the trainer very happy, since Nikka weighs over three hundred pounds, and her claws are almost three inches long!

IN THE WILD, LIONS USE THEIR LARGE CLAWS TO HOLD THEIR PREY TIGHTLY.

A CAT'S MOLARS CAN CUT MEAT THE WAY SCISSORS DO.

From the day you get your kitten, you must teach her not to bite. Even a little "nip" during playtime when she's very young should not be allowed. Every time your kitten opens her mouth close to any part of your body, say a firm "No." Soon she will learn that biting at any time is off-limits.

A RIVER OTTER HAS THIRTY-
SIX SHARP TEETH THAT IT
USES TO CATCH FOOD.

Otters must be taught not to bite
when they are very young. Unless
they learn this well, their trainers
can receive nasty bites while caring
for them. Since this otter, Cajun,
knows never to bite his trainer,
playtime is a lot of fun.

25

A CAT CAN LEAP MORE THAN SIX FEET OFF THE GROUND.

You need to teach your kitten to stay off tables and countertops where your family eats and prepares food. When you first see your kitten climb up on the counter, say a stern "No" and lift him off. If you do this every time your kitten tries to get on the counters and tables, he will soon understand that they are off-limits.

Because of elephants' tremendous weight, they are taught to be careful and not step on things they could break. This elephant, Judy, knows to avoid stepping on picnic tables and other objects as she and her trainer go for long walks in the park.

THE AFRICAN ELEPHANT IS THE LARGEST LAND MAMMAL IN THE WORLD. IT WEIGHS MORE THAN THIRTEEN

WHEN KITTENS SCRATCH
THEIR SCRATCHING POSTS,
THE OUTER PART OF THEIR
OLD WORN-OUT CLAWS
STRIPS OFF TO REVEAL BRAND
NEW CLAWS UNDERNEATH.

It is natural for your kitten to scratch things, and it helps to keep her claws healthy. But it is important to teach her to scratch on a scratching post, *not* on the furniture. Place the post wherever she is most active. If you see her scratching on anything else, say a stern "No" and take her to the post immediately.

If she continues to try to scratch the furniture, tape wax paper on those areas of the furniture she seems to like best. She won't like the wax paper, and will soon learn not to scratch the furniture. Always give your kitten lots of praise when she uses her scratching post.

Orangutans are very strong and can cause a lot of damage, so they are taught to respect things around them when they are very young. This trainer gives Jolynn a sturdy toy with which she can be as rough as she wants to be, in the same way your kitten has its scratching post.

IN THE WILD, ORANGUTANS LIVE IN TREES AND WILL RARELY COME DOWN TO THE GROUND.

CATS CAN FIND THEIR
WAY HOME FROM SHORT
DISTANCES BECAUSE THEY
HAVE AN EXCELLENT MEMORY
FOR EVERYTHING THEY SEE,
AND ARE ASSISTED BY
FAMILIAR SCENTS.

You can train your kitten to greet you at the door when you get home. Every time you open the door, jiggle it so your kitten can hear it, and say "Come" loudly. (Your kitten should already know the command "Come" before you teach him this.) Have treats and lots of praise ready to give your kitten as soon as he comes. If you do this every time you get home, your kitten will soon learn to meet you at the door whenever he hears you coming.

These dolphins enjoy being with their trainers very much. Every time the trainers come near the pool, the dolphins dart over to greet them, just as your kitten can greet you at the door. The dolphins are always excited to see their trainers, because they know their arrival means a fun training session, playtime, a tasty fish, or a rubdown!

IN THE WILD, DOLPHINS LIVE IN GROUPS CALLED PODS. THERE MAY BE A DOZEN, OR UP TO SEVERAL HUNDRED, DOLPHINS IN EACH POD.

THE FATTEST KNOWN HOUSE CAT WAS FROM ENGLAND. TIGER WEIGHED FORTY-THREE POUNDS. (HE DID NOT PLAY FETCH!)

Kittens can learn to fetch things just as well as any puppy can. Fetch is a good game to teach your kitten, and a great way to help her stay fit. Start by setting a soft toy right below your kitten's mouth. When your kitten picks the toy up, say "Give it," and gently take the toy back from your kitten. After your kitten starts giving the soft toy back to you each time, throw it a short distance and tell your kitten to "Fetch." Increase the distance you throw the toy each time.

It is important to tell your kitten to "Give it" whenever you ask for the soft toy back. You will then be able to use this command anytime your kitten has something in her mouth you want her to give you, such as a bug, a sharp object, or your homework.

Sea lions love to play fetch by swimming out to bring something back for their trainers. It's a great way for the sea lions to stay fit and alert.

SEA LIONS CAN SWIM AT SPEEDS OF UP TO FIFTEEN MILES PER HOUR.

YOUR KITTEN'S STRONGEST SENSE IS SIGHT; HEARING IS ITS SECOND STRONGEST SENSE.

If your cat spends a lot of time outside, you will want to teach him to come *inside*, where it's safe, for the night. You can do this by saving his last feeding for the evening.

Start by giving a signal every time you feed him, such as tapping the can of food with a spoon. Your kitten will soon learn the sound that means "dinnertime!" Then, when he's old enough to start going outside, he will always come inside for the night at your special signal.

34

IN THE WILD, TIGERS CAN EAT UP TO FORTY POUNDS IN A DAY, THEN EAT NOTHING FOR THE NEXT COUPLE OF DAYS.

Rakon loves dinnertime so much that his trainers never had to teach him a special signal. Rakon learned his own signal for dinnertime! Every time he hears the refrigerator door opening behind the fence of his large grassy home, he wakes up and runs to his trainer for a tasty carton of milk.

CATS ARE NOT COMPLETELY
COLOR-BLIND. THEY CAN TELL
THE DIFFERENCE BETWEEN
SHADES OF RED AND GREEN.

You can teach your kitten to jump up on your lap and spend some quiet time with you. Settle yourself in a comfortable chair, and have some treats ready. While your kitten is on the floor next to you, show your kitten the treat, and say "Up." Give your kitten the treat and a lot of praise when she jumps onto your lap. Repeat this several times until your kitten understands the command "Up." This is a nice way to spend time with your kitten.

and critters, too!

IN THE WILD, SQUIRREL
MONKEYS LIVE IN TREES
IN GROUPS OF UP TO A
HUNDRED.

This trainer teaches Baxter to jump
up on his arm the exact same way
you train your kitten to jump up on
your lap. The monkey wears a har-
ness and a leash to help the trainer
keep control. After all the time
these two have spent in training
sessions together, they have a very
special friendship.

37

WHEN YOUR KITTEN PURRS, THIS IS A SIGNAL IT IS IN A FRIENDLY SOCIAL MOOD.

While training your kitten, you will spend a lot of time together and be able to share many family activities. The learning sessions will build a bond between the two of you that you can't develop any other way. Through training your kitten, you will establish a very special lifelong relationship.

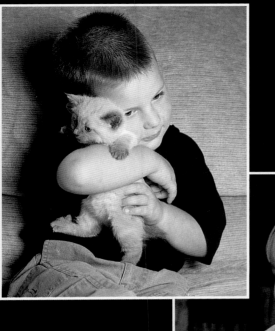

Printed in Hong Kong by South China Printing Company (1988) Ltd.
The text type is Century Light.

Library of Congress Cataloging in Publication Data
Petersen-Fleming, Judy. Kitten training and critters, too! / by Judy Petersen-Fleming
and Bill Fleming ; photographs by Darryl Bush. — 1st ed.   p. cm. Summary: Shows
how to train a kitten by drawing comparisons with the ways in which keepers
train wild animals in captivity.
1. Kittens—Training—Juvenile literature. 2. Animal training—Juvenile literature.
[1. Cats—Training. 2. Animal training.] I. Fleming, Bill. II. Bush, Darryl, ill. III. Title.
SF446.6.P47 1996 636.8'0887—dc20 95-665 CIP AC
ISBN 0-688-13386-X (trade).—ISBN 0-688-13387-8 (lib. bdg.)

1 3 5 7 9 10 8 6 4 2
First edition

Photographs on pages 10, 16, 22, 26, 28, and 30 copyright © 1996 by Debra Reingold-Reiss.
All other photographs copyright © 1996
by Darryl W. Bush/Marine World Africa USA, Vallejo, California.